POEMS
ON THE
UNDERGROUND
96

edited by
Gerard Benson
Judith Chernaik
Cicely Herbert

CASSELL

Cassell Publishers Limited
Wellington House, 125 Strand
London WC2R 0BB

First published 1996

British Library Cataloguing in Publication Data
A catalogue record for this book is available from the British Library

ISBN 0–304–34857–0

Typeset in Monotype Meridien by
KDI, Newton le Willows, Lancs.

Printed and bound in Great Britain by
Hillman Printers Ltd

CONTENTS

THE POEMS

displayed on the London Underground
during 1996

To My Dear and Loving Husband

If ever two were one, then surely we.
If ever man were loved by wife, then thee;
If ever wife was happy in a man,
Compare with me ye women if you can.
I prize thy love more than whole mines of gold,
Or all the riches that the East doth hold.
My love is such that rivers cannot quench,
Nor ought but love from thee give recompence.
Thy love is such I can no way repay,
The heavens reward thee manifold I pray.
Then while we live, in love let's so persever,
That when we live no more, we may live ever.

ANNE BRADSTREET (1612–72)

Chorus from a Play

(written in the year 1700)

All, all, of a piece throughout;
Thy chase had a beast in view;
Thy wars brought nothing about;
Thy lovers were all untrue.
'Tis well an old age is out,
And time to begin a new.

JOHN DRYDEN (1631–1700)

Inversnaid

This dárksome búrn, hórseback brówn,
His rollrock highroad roaring down,
In coop and in comb the fleece of his foam
Flutes and low to the lake falls home.

A windpuff-bónnet of fáwn-fróth
Turns and twindles over the broth
Of a pool so pitchblack, féll-frówning,
It rounds and rounds Despair to drowning.

Degged with dew, dappled with dew
Are the groins of the braes that the brook treads through,
Wiry heathpacks, flitches of fern,
And the beadbonny ash that sits over the burn.

What would the world be, once bereft
Of wet and of wildness? Let them be left,
O let them be left, wildness and wet;
Long live the weeds and the wilderness yet.

GERARD MANLEY HOPKINS (1844–89)

A 14-Year-Old Convalescent Cat in the Winter

I want him to have another living summer,
to lie in the sun and enjoy the *douceur de vivre* –
because the sun, like golden rum in a rummer,
is what makes an idle cat *un tout petit peu ivre* –

I want him to lie stretched out, contented,
revelling in the heat, his fur all dry and warm,
an Old Age Pensioner, retired, resented
by no one, and happinesses in a beelike swarm

to settle on him – postponed for another season
that last fated hateful journey to the vet
from which there is no return (and age the reason),
which must soon come – as I cannot forget.

GAVIN EWART (1916–95)

Saturday Morning

Everyone who made love the night before
was walking around with flashing red lights
on top of their heads – a white-haired old gentleman,
a red-faced schoolboy, a pregnant woman
who smiled at me from across the street
and gave a little secret shrug,
as if the flashing red light on her head
was a small price to pay for what she knew.

HUGO WILLIAMS (b. 1942)

The Undertaking

The darkness lifts, imagine, in your lifetime.
There you are – cased in clean bark you drift
through weaving rushes, fields flooded with cotton.
You are free. The river films with lilies,
shrubs appear, shoots thicken into palm. And now
all fear gives way: the light
looks after you, you feel the waves' goodwill
as arms widen over the water; Love,

the key is turned. Extend yourself –
it is the Nile, the sun is shining,
everywhere you turn is luck.

LOUISE GLÜCK (b. 1943)

His Return to London

From the dull confines of the drooping West,
To see the day spring from the pregnant East,
Ravished in spirit, I come, nay more, I fly
To thee, blest place of my nativity!
Thus, thus with hallowed foot I touch the ground,
With thousand blessings by thy fortune crowned.
O fruitful Genius! that bestowest here
An everlasting plenty, year by year.
O place! O people! Manners! framed to please
All nations, customs, kindreds, languages!
I am a free-born Roman; suffer then,
That I amongst you live a citizen.
London my home is: though by hard fate sent
Into a long and irksome banishment;
Yet since called back; henceforward let me be,
O native country, repossessed by thee!
For, rather than I'll to the West return,
I'll beg of thee first here to have mine urn.
Weak I am grown, and must in short time fall;
Give thou my sacred relics burial.

ROBERT HERRICK (1591–1674)

'So we'll go no more a-roving'

So we'll go no more a-roving
　　So late into the night,
Though the heart be still as loving,
　　And the moon be still as bright.

For the sword outwears its sheath,
　　And the soul wears out the breast,
And the heart must pause to breathe,
　　And Love itself have rest.

Though the night was made for loving,
　　And the day returns too soon,
Yet we'll go no more a-roving
　　By the light of the moon.

GEORGE GORDON, LORD BYRON (1788–1824)

'I taste a liquor never brewed'

I taste a liquor never brewed –
From Tankards scooped in Pearl –
Not all the Vats upon the Rhine
Yield such an Alcohol!

Inebriate of Air – am I –
And Debauchee of Dew –
Reeling – thro endless summer days –
From inns of Molten Blue –

When "Landlords" turn the drunken Bee
Out of the Foxglove's door –
When Butterflies – renounce their "drams" –
I shall but drink the more!

Till Seraphs swing their snowy Hats –
And Saints – to windows run –
To see the little Tippler
Leaning against the – Sun –

EMILY DICKINSON (1830–86)

The Poet

Therefore he no more troubled the pool of silence.
But put on mask and cloak,
Strung a guitar
And moved among the folk.
Dancing they cried,
'Ah, how our sober islands
Are gay again, since this blind lyrical tramp
Invaded the Fair!'

Under the last dead lamp
When all the dancers and masks had gone inside
His cold stare
Returned to its true task, interrogation of silence.

GEORGE MACKAY BROWN (1921–96)

Greenwich Park

Spring's come, a little late, in the park:
a tree-rat smokes flat S's over the lawn.
A mallard has somehow forgotten something
it can't quite remember. Daffodils yawn,
prick their ears, push their muzzles out
for a kiss. Pansies spoof pensive
Priapus faces: Socrates or Verlaine.
A cock-pigeon is sexually harassing
a hen: pecking and poking and padding
behind her impertinently, bowing and mowing.
But when he's suddenly absent-minded –
can't keep even sex in his head –
she trembles, stops her gadding, doubts
and grazes his way. He remembers and pouts.

HERBERT LOMAS (b. 1924)

Apology

Humming your Nocturne on the Circle Line,
unlike the piano, running out of breath

I've been writing you out of my life
my loves (one out, one in).

I've pushed you out of the way to see
what the gaps in my life might look like,

how large they are,
how quickly I could write them in;

and not (at least till I've lost you both)
rewriting you only means

that the spaces I'm not writing in are where
I live.

MIMI KHALVATI (b. 1944)

'Under the greenwood tree'

Under the greenwood tree
Who loves to lie with me,
And turn his merry note
Unto the sweet bird's throat,
Come hither, come hither, come hither:
    Here shall he see
    No enemy
But winter and rough weather.

Who doth ambition shun
And loves to live i' th' sun,
Seeking the food he eats,
And pleased with what he gets,
Come hither, come hither, come hither:
    Here shall he see
    No enemy
But winter and rough weather.

from AS YOU LIKE IT

WILLIAM SHAKESPEARE (1564–1616)

from Poetry

And it was at that age . . . Poetry arrived
in search of me. I don't know, I don't know where
it came from, from winter or a river.
I don't know how or when,
no, they were not voices, they were not
words, nor silence,
but from a street I was summoned,
from the branches of night,
abruptly from the others,
among violent fires
or returning alone,
there I was without a face
and it touched me.

Y fue a esa edad . . . Llegó la poesía
a buscarme. No sé, no sé de dónde
salió, de invierno o río.
No sé cómo ni cuándo,
no, no eran voces, no eran
palabras, ni silencio,
pero desde una calle me llamaba,
desde las ramas de la noche,
de pronto entre los otros,
entre fuegos violentos
o regresando solo,
alli estaba sin rostro
y me tocaba.

PABLO NERUDA (1904–73)
translated by ALASTAIR REID

Memory of my Father

Every old man I see
Reminds me of my father
When he had fallen in love with death
One time when sheaves were gathered.

That man I saw in Gardner Street
Stumble on the kerb was one,
He stared at me half-eyed,
I might have been his son.

And I remember the musician
Faltering over his fiddle
In Bayswater, London,
He too set me the riddle.

Every old man I see
In October-coloured weather
Seems to say to me:
'I was once your father.'

PATRICK KAVANAGH (1906–67)

Secret Lives

Sometimes your dressing gown unhooks
and slides out under the garden door,
with three aces up his sleeve.

He flies in the face of next door's dog,
and backflips down the middle of the street,
opening himself and humming.

Something in pink nylon flutters at him
from a bedroom window. He twirls his cord
to beckon her outside.

They're heading for a club they know
where the dress code is relaxed midweek,
and the music is strictly soul.

SIÂN HUGHES

Potosí

The moon falls
like a metaphysician
on the silver city

so distressed a metal –
even the horses shod with silver
in the freezing streets

wagons, blue with graffiti
under the spoil-tips,
and at first light

mountain foxes,
red as cinnabar,
moving against the flow

between the silver-bearing lodes,
the upland snow.

PAULINE STAINER

The Lesson (an anti-pastoral)

The small schoolgirl
on her way down
grey Portugal Lane
late for class
who brushes a careless
hand against
the one green
nettle that had to sprout
from yards of concrete
can't believe
there's no dock leaf
to cancel
it out.

TRACY RYAN

NOTES TO THE POEMS

9   **To My Dear and Loving Husband**   Anne Bradstreet grew up in the household of the Earl of Lincoln, where her father Thomas Dudley, an ardent Puritan, was steward. In 1630, when she was 18, she emigrated to the Massachusetts Bay Colony with her husband Simon Bradstreet and her father, each of whom later became Governor of the colony. Her poems were published in England in 1650, as *The Tenth Muse Lately Sprung Up in America*.

10   **Chorus from a Play**   From *The Secular Masque*, one of the last works written by Dryden, in which he satirizes a century riven by religious war.

11   **Inversnaid**   Dated September 28, 1881. Burn: a small river or stream. The Snaid burn runs from Loch Arklet to the tiny hamlet of Inversnaid, where it enters Loch Lomond. After seven weeks' service in the Glasgow slums as assistant at St Joseph's Church, Hopkins visited Loch Lomond and spent a few hours at Inversnaid. Several of the unfamiliar terms in the poem are his own coinage.

12   **A 14-Year-Old Convalescent Cat in the Winter**   Gavin Ewart, one of the most delightful writers of light verse of our time, supported Poems on the Underground from its inception, sending us a poem a day in our first few months. A genial presence at our poetry readings and workshops, his 'Convalescent Cat' was one of the most popular poems ever to appear on the Tube.

15   **His Return to London**   Having remained loyal to Charles I, Herrick was ejected in 1647 from his post as vicar at Dean Prior, Devon, and retired to London, where he remained until 1660. For reasons of space we had to use a shortened version of the poem on the Tube.

16   **'So we'll go no more a-roving'**   Written in a letter to Thomas Moore in which Byron admits to over-indulging in carnival festivities: 'The mumming closed with a masked ball at the Fenice, where I went, as also to most of the ridottos, etc., etc., and, though I did not dissipate much upon the whole, yet I find "the sword wearing out the scabbard", though I have but just turned the corner of twenty-nine.'

ACKNOWLEDGEMENTS

George Mackay Brown: 'The Poet' from *Selected Poems 1954–1983*, © George Mackay Brown 1991. Reprinted by permission of John Murray.

Gavin Ewart: 'A 14-Year-Old Convalescent Cat in the Winter' from *The New Ewart: Poems 1980–1982*, © Gavin Ewart 1982. Reprinted by permission of Hutchinson.

Louise Glück: 'The Undertaking' from *The House on Marshland*, © Louise Glück 1975. Reprinted by permission of Ecco Press.

Siân Hughes: 'Secret Lives', © Siân Hughes 1996. Printed by permission of the author.

Patrick Kavanagh: 'Memory of my Father' from *The Complete Poems of Patrick Kavanagh*, © Peter Kavanagh 1972. Reprinted by permission of Peter Kavanagh.

Mimi Khalvati: 'Apology' from *Mirrorwork*, © Mimi Khalvati 1995. Reprinted by permission of Carcanet Press.

Herbert Lomas: 'Greenwich Park' from *Selected Poems*, © Herbert Lomas 1995. Reprinted by permission of the author.

Pablo Neruda: 'Poetry' from 'La poesia' translated by Alastair Reid, *Pablo Neruda, Selected Poems*, ed. Nathaniel Tarn, © Pablo Neruda 1970. Reprinted by permission of Jonathan Cape.

Tracy Ryan: 'The Lesson (an anti-pastoral)', © Tracy Ryan 1966. Printed by permission of the author.

Pauline Stainer: 'Potosí', © Pauline Stainer 1996. Printed by permission of the author.

Hugo Williams: 'Saturday Morning' from *Dock Leaves*, © Hugo Williams 1994. Reprinted by permission of Faber and Faber.

A NOTE OF THANKS

'Poems on the Underground' would like to thank London Transport for continuing support for the programme during 1996. We are also grateful to the London Arts Board, the British Library (Stefan Zweig Programme) and the British Council, which arranged special displays of poems from our collection in Helsinki and Oslo during 1995–96. The Autumn display of poems was made possible by *The Times Literary Supplement*, through their sponsorship of the first TLS/Poems on the Underground Poetry Competition. We owe special thanks to Tom Davidson, who designed the posters.

Readers may like to know that copies of the Underground poem posters can be purchased from the London Transport Museum, Freepost, Covent Garden, London WC2E 7BB.